No Safe Place

CHRISTA HERNANDEZ

1.888.5069-NOW
www.nowscpress.com
 @nowscpress

Ordering Information:

Quantity sales. Special discounts are available on quantity purchases by corporations, associations, and others. For details, contact the publisher at the address above.

Orders by U.S. trade bookstores and wholesalers. Please contact: NOW SC Press: Tel: (888) 5069-NOW or visit www. nowscpress.com.

Printed in the United States of America

First Printing, 2017

ISBN: 978-0-9995845-2-1

Dedication

This book is dedicated first and foremost to my children! Thank you for never giving up on me and still loving me even in my darkest times. To my sweet granddaughter, you have helped me to become the person I am today and have given me a second chance to make right choices with you, choices that I didn't know how to give your mom and uncle. To my family, I love you all, even through our dysfunction. I know this is only the beginning for all of us.

Mom, I love you and want you to always remember you are forgiven. Not just by me, but by our Heavenly Father. Love you!

To each and every person reading this book, especially my sisters and brothers in the commercial sex industry and those who are being trafficked or have been, I love you all and wrote this book to bring you hope in your darkest places and to let you know you are loved beyond measure, right where you are. There are people fighting for you and there is light at the end of the tunnel. What has been done for me can and will be done for you.

For anyone reading this, please know "You can do hard things," so keep moving forward and never give up on your dreams! There is a great plan for your life!

Table of Contents

Part Three: Building Home

Foreword

In 2013, as the new Pastor for Outreach and Ministry at St. Andrews Presbyterian Church, I was asking God to show me who some of the most vulnerable people in our community were and how we could reach them. I had been praying about it for days, and as I drove past the illuminated sign of one of the many clubs, both a thought and an idea suddenly popped into my head. The women in those clubs are vulnerable. The women in those clubs need to know that they are loved and that they matter to God. That was the thought, and then I had the idea. Maybe we could go into those places and take gifts for the women as a sign of love and a reminder of their worth. The idea was immediately followed by questions that I had no idea how to answer. *Is that even possible? Would clubs let us in? What would we say?* When I got home, I got on the computer to see if I could find anyone anywhere doing something like. I discovered the Treasures website, which included a map showing places where ministries like theirs existed. There was a dot in Tampa with an email address. I wrote to the woman, telling her about my idea and asked if she could offer any insight or guidance. The woman was Christa and a few days later, I met her for the first time at a Starbucks.

I knew on the day that I met Christa that she was the real thing, meaning that I could see that she was a woman who had been transformed by Jesus in a miraculous way and that she had a vision that God was bound to bless. Even though I had never set foot in a strip club, and wasn't sure if anyone in my congregation would follow me down that road, I wanted to be part of what Christa was doing. I wanted to go into those clubs with her because I felt sure that Jesus would go there. Ultimately, I did go with Christa and many in my congregation went with me, because they also wanted to reach these women that God loves. It has been a joy and a rare privilege to support and to learn from Christa in these recent years.

As we have served and worked together over these last few years, I have had the chance to hear much of Christa's story and to witness her transformed life. When I read in greater detail what she has experienced and what she has survived, I can see even more clearly why she is so driven in ministry and so passionate about going back into the clubs to help those who are in the same situation she used to be in. She understands firsthand that the darkness is powerful but also knows firsthand that the light that she brings is ultimately more powerful than darkness.

I'm thankful that she has written this book so that many more people will have the opportunity to see the miracle that her life is and to learn from her. For those on the outside of the clubs and industry life, Christa's story is an eye-opening account that reveals the truth about why many women "choose" the sex industry, not as a profession but as a way to survive. It is also an important reminder that women working in the sex industry are not objects or enemies. They are real people, with real stories, real hurts, and real hopes and like anyone they need love, opportunities, support, and real friendship. For those on the inside who will recognize Christa's story because their own is something like it, Christa offers a message of hope and a vision of what is possible. For those inside the church, Christa's story reminds us that grace opens doors that our short-sighted and careless judgments often close, and for those outside of the church there is a clear message that no matter where you are, God is for you and God loves you unconditionally.

Rev. Joy W. Laughridge
Associate Pastor
St. Andrews Presbyterian Church, Dunedin, FL

Part One:
Losing Home

Chapter One

Home of Shattered Dreams

The music is pounding so loud that it shakes the floor. Smoke fills the air, leaving a hazy film over the entire space. On the stage, a trio of women — thin, heavy, dark, light — slither against poles with a bored, pained look in their eyes.

I know that look. I'm familiar with that pain. I've been there, been on that pole, and for a while, I thought I'd never escape. I've never been the kind of person God could love.

I move through the room, and hand each of the girls working the floor a cute little zebra patterned bag with pink tissue paper, an eyeshadow pallet, lip gloss, and a business card that simply says: *You are loved. You have a purpose. We are here.*

One of the girls — a thin blonde with heavy eye makeup in a short, tight, sequined dress — hurries after me. "Can we talk?" she asks.

We duck into the dressing room and sit across from each other in torn, battered chairs that are sticky with hairspray and makeup. The wall-length mirror is sparsely lit, and there is a jumble of makeup and curling irons along the scarred counter.

I wait for her to talk. I know how hard these first words are to speak.

"Why are you here?" she asks. "Why do you care about us?"

I reach for her hand, just one light touch; "Because I was you once."

Because I was you once.

It takes a moment for her to see, for her to understand. Tears well in her eyes and she fiddles with the business card. "No one has ever told someone like me that I matter."

"You do," I say. "More than you know." I pause again, waiting, and when she doesn't speak, I open that door for her. "Tell me about your life."

"My life...has been hell. For as long as I can remember." And she begins to tell me about being abandoned as a child when her parents divorced, about being abused and treated like Tuesday's trash, and about how that led to her being on a stage, scrambling for dollar bills and losing a little more of her dignity every day.

"I get it," I say, and then I begin to tell her about me. About how I went from a little girl with pigtails and a favorite stuffed bear to a woman being sold to men who saw me as nothing more than a momentary thrill. As the story pours out of me, I begin to forgive myself a little more and give the girl across from me a ray of hope that maybe her life can change, too.

My first memory of my parents is hearing about how my father tied my mother to a tree, threatening to kill her. He beat her at the dinner table once because the gravy was lumpy. He beat her for reading a romance novel. My mother, who had grown up in a religious community where she was beaten with a two-by-four, maybe didn't know any other kind of life. Every element of her childhood was controlled by her psychotically religious father.

My grandfather (my mother's father) had a compound in Georgia where he used mind control to get his followers pumped up about his religion, while they slaved away on his property. The men were in charge, and the women wore ankle-length, Amish-style dresses, kept their hair long and wore absolutely no makeup. I remember visiting him once, and while we sat at his long oak dinner table, eating eggs from the chicken coop and drinking milk straight from a cow, he told us a story about the time when my mother wouldn't eat as a child, and he reached over to stab her with a fork. My mother grew up with her own wounds that never seemed to heal.

My father was adopted by a Cuban woman named Betsy, who raised him in a dingy little bar where fights would break out and he would see drunks fighting and my grandma grabbing her good old baseball bat to chase them out.

My maternal grandmother, or MawMaw as I called her, divorced her religious cult husband and remarried a man I called PawPaw. He was one of the first employees at the contemporary resort in Disney World, and when I was little, my grandparents bought me frilly little dresses and took me to Disney World often. My mother said her parents treated me like a porcelain doll and never let me wear the same dress twice.

I just loved my PawPaw. There was something especially safe about him. We lived right across the street from them, and life in those first few years of my life was good. My parents had their own business, an upscale hair salon.

When I turned three, my little brother was born on my birthday. A year later, my mother had my second little brother. That was the year I began to notice my father had strange thoughts. I remember my father, who was an ordained minister of the Alpha and Omega Church, swore one of the elder's spirits was in the room when my little brother was conceived, which meant he would grow up to be a preacher. My father also insisted all of our names be a form of the word Christ, which turned out to be a very ironic choice, given the kind of man my father was.

I have mixed memories of my childhood; happy afternoons when my brothers and I ran back and forth from MawMaw and PawPaw, swimming in the big above ground pool in their back yard, and then coming home for lunch.

But there were also dark days like the day my father drove to my grandparents' house with my mother's head rolled up in the window, while she cried from the pain. At another time when we were on our way to church and were driving around a lake, something set my father off. He started hitting my mother, then pulled over and shoved her out of the car like he was throwing trash on the side of the road.

My father controlled what my mother wore, how her hair and make-up were done, and even how she dressed me. As a little girl, I would see my mom sobbing, and would feel helpless because I couldn't help her. My mother was always nervous, always walking on eggshells, never knowing what would blow up next.

When I was five, my parents sat me down separately and said they were getting a divorce. Each of them asked me where I wanted to live. Even though home was like a ticking time bomb, there were good times and these were my parents. I loved them both dearly. I couldn't choose one over the other, and all I remember feeling is scared. I didn't know what divorce meant or what would happen to my brothers and me.

When the divorce came through, my father took everything he could from my mother. People in the town where we lived called my father "Little Hitler" because he always got what he wanted. This divorce was no different. He took all three of us and everything that wasn't nailed down. He left my mother with cardboard boxes filled with her belongings cut into shreds. He had her arrested for abandoning us and I remember my father laughing at her on the courthouse stairs.

Laughing at her on the courthouse stairs.

My father moved us into a two-bedroom duplex. I remember long nights at the babysitter's, lying on a pallet in front of an old TV watching shows like *Happy Days*. The TV world seemed so unreal to me, because in the Cunningham home, the parents loved Ritchie and were united. While in my reality, our mother had been forbidden to see us.

I also began to see another darker side of the world. There were a group of older boys who lived in the duplex across the street. They would set up tents and I remember them luring me in to play house with them. I was too little to know what to do when they touched me. I felt violated but never said anything to my parents in fear that it was somehow my fault and I would get in trouble.

When I was in first grade, my parents got back together for a brief time. We were so happy to have our mom back in the home. It seemed as though things were getting better. But that didn't last long.

One night, a man came to the door, enraged, because my father had raped his brother with a wooden peg leg. My mother was horrified when she confronted my father, and she told him this time it was truly over between them. Something ripped out of my little heart.

After my mother left again, things started to get stranger with dad. He had become a licensed hypnotist and set up a room in the back of the hair salon to have sessions. Whenever he took me in that room, he would turn on this machine and have me look at a black and white image spinning while listening to his voice speak in a very slow, low tone. My eyes got heavy, and every time I tried to fight the urge to fall under the hypnosis, I couldn't. I would play along, too young to know what he could hide by hypnotizing me.

My mother remarried and soon had a baby girl. Her new husband wasn't the nicest man. I can still hear "bend over and grab your ankles" so he could beat us without our hands getting in the way. I would have the nastiest black and blue bruises that lasted for days and days.

I didn't see my mother very often, so when it was time to go to her house, I'd get nervous and giddy. Even though my stepfather could be mean sometimes, it was a whole different atmosphere in their house. We would hang out like a family, running around the cul-de-sac, sitting with my stepfather's friends while they shucked oysters, or watching amateur car racing at the track where my stepfather had a car.

My father, however, hated us going to Mom's house. If we cried when we came home (because we didn't want to leave Mom's), he would yell at us and tell us that Mom was bad for us. He said I had an unhealthy attachment to her. I guess in some ways I did because I craved seeing her, craved something — anything — consistent in my life.

I remember sitting on my knees by the screen door waiting for our mom to come, but she rarely did. We would cry because she wasn't there, and Dad would get mad at us for crying. It was a vicious cycle.

There are only a few happy times I remember with my father. I loved it when he took us to the beach. We would swim out to the sandbar in search of starfish and play in the white sand. On the way home, we would always stop off and get smoked mullet. Sometimes he took us fishing with our cane poles and bobbers.

One winter, he took us on a vacation to the Smoky Mountains in our old beat-up station wagon. Dad pulled over to the side of the road so we could make a snowman. Before we got out, the car began to slide, until it was literally teeter-tottering off the edge of the mountain. My father told each of us to get out, slowly and one by one. When it was over and a tow truck had pulled the car back from the edge, Dad hugged us and told us how much he loved us. I wanted to hold on to that moment, but it disappeared as quickly as raindrops on hot pavement. Before long, my father was back to pulling over to spank us for being too loud or bickering in the back seat.

It disappeared as quickly as raindrops on hot pavement.

I have so few other memories of my childhood. I remember these little snippets, I remember the Raggedy Ann and Andy wallpaper in my room, but there are other huge blank spaces in my childhood. It was during those years that I learned to dissociate, which was compounded by my father's hypnosis "game".

I was so young, and already such a broken little girl. I couldn't understand why my life was so different from the lives of my friends, the lives I saw on TV. I had two dads (my dad and his lover) and a mom I barely got to see. I was beaten, threatened and shed more tears than I can count. I felt so alone, and so sure that God did not love our family — or love me. He was there — He was always there — and when I look back, I see the ways that God tried to reach me and comfort me.

Chapter Two

The Haunted House

The girl in the strip club listened to my story and the distrust in her eyes slowly gave way to faith. We talked until the manager came in and told her to get back on stage. I watched her leave the dressing room, the hope she'd had for a moment gone, and I prayed that the next time I came here, I could convince her that she, like me, was worth saving. Then I moved on to the next place, with another set of makeup bags and business cards, found another girl with runny makeup and despair in her eyes, and began to talk again.

I was around ten years old when we made a move to an old house with wooden floors that creaked when you walked across them. It was only a two bedroom; so for a while, my little brothers and I shared a room. Eventually, my father made the raggedy little back porch into a roach-infested kitchen and the old kitchen into his and his boyfriend's bedroom. We had a huge backyard where my dad built a garden and a shed that we pretended was a clubhouse. From the outside, that little house on Lime Street looked normal. Inside, it was a house of horrors.

My bedroom became the old master bedroom. I was terrified of that room. It was full of windows and had these long sheer curtains that would blow to the ceiling, but still, I felt this dark presence in it.

My father had some strange friends who were into astrology and hypnosis. They would sit around our dining room table, "communicating" with the other side. They'd set a silver cone-shaped thing they called a trumpet in the middle of the table. When they would start talking to the spiritual world, that thing would start moving.

I wasn't scared of someone breaking in; I was scared of what I couldn't see and whatever was moving that trumpet around during their séances. One night, my father brought me to one of their "meetings".

We went to this building by a lake. Everyone was sitting in a candlelit circle on the floor, with something shaped like a star in the middle. I sat beside my father, and then everyone started chanting. My father's blue eyes turned black and he told me that the spirit he called his guide started talking through him. "Child, I was once young like you and scared but you have nothing to be afraid of."

I don't even know what happened next. That's where the memory ends. I don't remember leaving that place, our ride home, nothing. All I know is that it left me even more terrified of that house and those strange friends. I later found out my father was the leader of a satanic group, and there was also a blood sacrifice made over me from a goat. They spoke horrible things over me, claiming I would be the bride of Satan and a server of man. It may have been at that meeting when the sacrifice was made.

Then the physical abuse began. My father wouldn't arrive home until late so it was us and Ralph, his boyfriend. He would beat us with this skinny belt. My father preferred switches. I remember one time he beat my brothers with a branch from a rose bush until they were bleeding.

I learned to disassociate from the abuse, which meant I could step outside myself and see the abuse as if it was happening to someone else. Despite this, my brothers and I tried to make happy memories of games of red light/green light in the back yard or melting Jolly Rancher candies over the old radiator heaters.

When the rickety church van came through the neighborhood, we'd go to church. I'd sit there, hearing all about God, and getting more confused every Sunday. This God wasn't the God I heard about at home. Still, I prayed every night:

This God wasn't the God I heard about at home.

Dear Jesus, please keep me, my friends, and family safe. Let me think of good things not bad things, happy things not sad things, and help me to have good dreams not bad dreams. Please forgive me for all my sins and if there's anything I haven't said, please fulfill it for me. I love you Jesus. Amen!

In the summer, we went to a recreation camp at my elementary school. Even there, I wasn't safe. One day, one of the workers molested me and another girl. I felt his hand sliding under my shirt, but I was frozen in fear and then he began to massage my barely budding breast. That afternoon broke me in ways none of the other stuff had, and I'm not really sure why. I remember walking home, and breaking down when I told Ralph.

My father pressed charges, and I remember wearing a pretty dress to go and do a deposition. But there wasn't enough evidence and the DA didn't prosecute him. This man got away with it. How could they not believe us and let this man go?

This man got away with it.

For a brief time, I went to live at my mother's house. When my mom saw huge

17

bruises on my bottom from my stepdad's punishment, she left him. But she was a weak woman when it came to men and took him back soon enough. Meanwhile, I began acting out with a boy next door. I was confused and lonely during those months.

I thought I was safe at my mom's house and had just begun to relax when my father took me back and I had to return to that house I was so scared of. It was like a game he played between my mom and I. He would wait until I was comfortable and then yank me back.

I protested and threw temper tantrums. My dad's response? He had me committed to a mental hospital. I was placed with the adults and spent almost every day there terrified. I remember one elderly woman wearing a straightjacket in her wheelchair. She would beg me to take it off her and when I would say no, she would spit on me. They had me feed her pudding in the dining room and she would spit that at me, too; it was horrible. I was just a scared little girl who wanted to go home.

In my counseling sessions, I told the doctor everything about that house of horrors, about being molested, about the abuse and about how much I wanted to live with my mother. I thought the doctor was a safe confidant but he wasn't. He brought my dad in and told him everything I had said. When it came time to go home, I prayed the doctor would send me to live with my mother, but the doctor told me I was sick for wanting a relationship with my mom so bad. He called it an unhealthy obsession and sent me home with my father.

I was beginning to think there were no safe people and that I was alone. The man who sexually abused me got away with it, and my father was even getting away with it. I kept thinking if there was a God, why wasn't he protecting me? How could my father speak of this God but do so many terrible things? I prayed and prayed, but felt alone and forgotten.

Chapter Three

Home of Disappointment

The blonde wasn't there the next time I stopped in, or the time after that. I began to worry that I had lost her to the streets, or to the sex trafficking world; lost her like I had once lost myself. But then, on the third week, she was there, and when she saw me, her eyes welled. "I've thought about your story a lot," she told me. "Can you tell me more?"

We sat in the dressing room again, the space now a carbon copy of the last time I'd been there, and I began to talk. I noticed the haunted look in her eyes, the shadows on her face, and prayed my words would somehow reach her and tell her she was loved. I had gone too many years not knowing that, and I wanted to spare her that pain.

When I was thirteen, we moved to a new house. I had such high hopes, but all we had done was trade one crappy situation for another crappy situation. I ended up sharing a room with my biracial sister — my mom had her with another man and had decided to give her up for adoption. My dad said no, that we already knew her as our sister, and he adopted her. Sometimes I wonder if it would have been better for her if she had gone with strangers.

Most of our clothes in those days came from Goodwill or the dollar store. I was in elementary school, and desperately trying to fit in. I peeled the Keds brand name off the back of a too-small pair of sneakers and glued it to the back of my dollar store ones. Still, I felt like an outcast in every way. I knew my family wasn't normal but unfortunately, it was the only normal I had.

It was the only normal I had.

For a while, I served as the school's safety patrol. I thought I was so cool with that orange vest and silver badge. I was somebody in that moment; I was important. Then my grades started dropping as the stress at home increased and I was taken off the safety patrol. I wanted so badly to tell someone about what was happening, but I knew if I did, it would only make things worse. I had been let down by authorities already — why risk that again?

Like many abused kids, I sought comfort in the familiar — the physical attention of another. I knew it wasn't right, but I didn't know any other way. One of the boys down the street would have me come over to his house and make out while rubbing on each other. One of my dad's friends had an older daughter who would touch me during sleepovers. By this time, I didn't know how to say no. There's something that happens in a child's brain when she is sexually abused — it creates this deep-seated belief that you deserve it, you asked for it. And the more the cycle continues, the more it reinforces that message.

At home, my dad got a new toy — a stun gun. It started off as a game to try to tag us, but like everything, quickly turned into a punishment.

He started recording all our calls, to make sure we weren't talking to our mother. We really didn't get to see her at all at this point. He would tell us to call our mother a bitch and liar whenever we talked to her on the phone. I refused to do it but my siblings had so much fear of what Dad might do that they fulfilled his bidding.

It was at that age when I started to rebel. One time, I tried to rewind the cassette tape on the recording device and erase a forbidden conversation I'd had with my mom, but my father found out and slapped my face so hard I fell down. We rolled around on that floor, fighting. I kneed him hard in his groin and he finally stopped. The next day, my face was bruised so badly I had to stay home from school and keep hamburger meat on my face. It was supposed to make the bruising go away faster, but that mark on my face stayed for days. As awful as that was, a part of me was glad to see the deep purple bruise on my father's groin.

I started fighting back, not only for me but also for my siblings. What did I have to lose at this point? Life was a constant storm of sexual abuse, physical abuse, mental abuse and spiritual abuse. Nobody else was going to protect us. Nobody else was going to save us.

I thought I was becoming one tough cookie but really, I was just building walls and protecting wounds that were too hard to handle. My father tried to swat down any rebellion he saw. Right before the 6th grade dance, he cut my curly hair until it looked like I had a giant poodle on my head. I snuck a hair clip and put it up once I got to the dance. But my father showed up early to get me and ripped that clip out of my hair, then beat me the whole way home. He had to have control of everything. Why?

We only had a few good memories in that house, like the time our neighbor threw a stolen pillowcase full of candy into our yard. Once in a while, we'd sneak down to the Babcock's at the end of the street where we could get a free hotdog and soda. These were the highlights of our life, the small bright spots in some very dark days.

Small bright spots in some very dark days.

I kept praying to God every night but my prayers were angry. I'd ask Him if He was real, why was this my life? Why couldn't we have been adopted? Why did He choose this family for us?

That phone call I had snuck to my mother told her things weren't good at my father's house. She called DCF, the Department of Children and Families, and I thought yes, finally, we were going to get out of this hellhole, and maybe God did hear me! We would be rescued. I was ready to tell them everything. I didn't care if we ended up going to Mom's or getting adopted. I just wanted us out of there.

Somehow, my father got wind before DCF showed up. He threatened us if we said a word to them, we'd be separated and thrown into foster care. Then he sealed it with that look that shot terror down our spines. It was enough to scare my siblings silent.

In the end, I kept my mouth shut, too. I couldn't risk being separated from my siblings. DCF left and there went our rescue. Dad started looking at new houses. He promised we were going to move into an even nicer house with a pool and pool table. He'd dialed back on the abuse for a while and I began to hope that maybe things were looking up. Wishful thinking!

I was allowed to spend a rare weekend with a friend. I called my mom, and she told me, "Christa, your father is packing a U-Haul and taking you kids far away."

I thought she was wrong, but when I got home, I saw the loaded U-Haul. A few hours later, we were all on our way to South Carolina.

It turned out that DCF had been suspicious and had started to build a case against my father. Instead of letting us go, he gave up his successful business and half his belongings to get us across state lines. In those days, DCF didn't track families that went to different states and no one knew where we were for well over a year. Why did he take us so far away to try and keep us only to abuse us more? I think because Little Hitler had to have control of everything.

I felt lost and defeated. And most of all, alone.

Chapter Four

Home of Changes

The blonde wasn't there every week. I understood that. I understood the flitting in and out of life, the reluctance to trust another person. But I kept going there, kept talking to the other girls. Every week, I asked about the blonde. The next time I saw her, I acted as if we'd seen each other the day before, not weeks before. I knew she had had enough shame and guilt in her life that she didn't need any from me, simply because she was struggling with believing she could be loved by another person, by God.

We sat down again, with some water and a couple pieces of chicken we took in. If we hadn't been surrounded by glitter and pounding music, we could have been ordinary friends out for an ordinary night, except we were having a conversation that was far from ordinary.

I started to tell her about the house in South Carolina that my father moved us into. I didn't even have a bed — my little sister and I slept on a used raggedy mattress. One of the springs took a chunk out of my leg, because the mattress was so crappy. We would wake up to mounds of poop and dog urine that would soak into the old wooden floors. Of course, it was our job to clean it before school and if it wasn't done like my father wanted it done, there was hell to pay.

I had to walk through the projects on my way home from school. Thugs would pull knives on me and I quickly had to learn to fight. I became the parent because my father and Ralph worked until late at night. It was our job to get dinner ready and clean the nasty house along with trying to get homework done. Half the time I was chasing after my siblings to do their part and stressing about anything being out of place because of the punishment I would receive. One night, my father knocked my youngest brother in the head and called him an idiot, because he didn't get the gravy right, just like I remember happening to Mom.

Whenever we would fight, we'd call Dad at the shop. Finally, he decided he would put an end to getting phone calls at work and chained my brothers to their wooden bunkbeds, leaving only enough length for them to get to the bathroom. We were living in the worst kind of hell and there was absolutely nothing I could do to help us.

We were living in the worst kind of hell.

I couldn't understand how there could be a God that would allow this. All of us felt deep shame and abandonment. We felt unlovable and that we must be horrible kids to have this happening to us. My father still had that recording device on the phone and when I talked to my friends, I'd use code words. It was so humiliating to have to tell my friends why my life was so abnormal.

In high school, I got my first job at a Waffle House. I worked the early morning shift on weekends and was finally able to purchase my own clothes. What a difference that made in my confidence. I hung out with some of the "in" crowd and was also in marching band, playing the clarinet.

We were back in contact with Mom. She'd tell us our father was an abomination to God for being gay and then send us a letter introducing her new girlfriend.

We were deprived of food often, eating ramen noodles and government cheese most days. But still my father got one of the first satellite dishes for himself. He got all the channels, including the porn channels. There were no parental controls and all of us kids watched it, and sometimes copied what we saw. We were humans with feelings that had already been awakened in us by the earlier abuses. I knew it was wrong, and even though it eventually stopped, I'm still working through the shame over this.

That sexual abuse led to acting out, as it does for so many children. My group of friends at school were taking bets on who would lose their virginity first. Even though I had been sexually abused, I had not had intercourse yet, and was technically still a virgin. I went to the house of one of the popular boys and lost my virginity to him, just to win the bet and even to be accepted. Losing my virginity wasn't really that big of a deal due to all I had been through. I was more thrilled about winning the bet. Word spread fast around school and the next thing I knew, one of the football players was inviting me to his house. I thought that was normal and what girls are supposed to do, so I had sex with him. I felt so accepted and like I had finally arrived, but all any of those boys wanted was a piece of me.

Normal and what girls are supposed to do.

I remember dating a boy from church. I was still able to catch the neighborhood bus to the Assembly of God Church from time to time. On our first date, we were five minutes late getting home. My dad was waiting in the bushes outside the house. When we pulled up, he terrified that boy so bad that he went speeding out of our driveway.

But it was worse when I got in the house. He told my siblings he was pulling my pants down to see if my pussy lips were swollen so he could see if I was out being a whore. When he did it, I was so mortified, but felt like it was my fault. I was a bad girl, and that was what bad girls got.

The next guy I dated, Bill, was my first puppy love. He was a guitar player in a Christian band and for some reason, my father liked him. I was allowed to go to his house and for those few hours, it was as if all my worries had disappeared. He was a senior and invited me to prom. I wore a royal blue strapless dress with white shoes. My dad took me to his house, his mom and my dad took lots of pictures, then we headed off in a limo. I felt like Cinderella. Not only was I with a guy I was head over heels in love with, but the friends we were with were some of the most popular kids in school. I wondered what they would think if they knew the real me, the hell I came from and the disgusting place I lived in, not to mention the horrible events in my past. But that night was magical and one of the best nights of my life.

His mom was great. I loved her and she loved me. I'd go out to their lake property with them sometimes, and had such a great time. I was truly away from it all with a real and normal family. I started opening up to his mom about some of the things going on in my home. They wanted to protect me but didn't know how. I think his mom called the state one time after my father beat me, but instead of it getting better, my father found out and banned me from seeing that boy anymore.

Banned me from seeing that boy anymore.

I failed ninth grade for missing too many days and for how low my grades were, so my dad decided to make me pay for my own tuition at a private Christian school. He thought this was also a way to get me away from that boy, but we still snuck around and saw each other. One night, we went to the movies and my dad found out. He dragged me out of there by my hair in front of everyone.

At that Christian school, I made friends with a girl named Shelly. She had a boyfriend and he had a friend, who went on to become my next boyfriend. Shelly had this cute little light blue Volkswagen that we would drive all over town in. On the weekends, I spent the night with her, and we often stayed up all night, tripping on acid while watching Pink Floyd with our boyfriends.

I became more and more promiscuous. I knew I needed birth control, and tried going to the counselor's office at school, like other girls had done. But the office called my father and from then on, I was only allowed out of the house for cheerleading practice. I got sent home for beating up the team captain one day and for some weird reason, my dad was proud of me and lightened up on my punishments.

I got caught one night for staying at a boy's house with Shelly. My father was so angry; I was terrified he might hurt me worse than ever this time. I pleaded for him to let me go stay at my mother's house in Florida. By this time, I was sixteen, and to my surprise, he said yes.

There was no tender goodbye with my father. He made me sign over my income tax refund to him, then had his partner hand me a pile of big black garbage bags for my belonging. He stayed in his room and told his boyfriend to take me to the Amtrak station with a one-way ticket to Florida. Part of me was relieved not to have another encounter with my father, but another part was very hurt.

Part Two: Finding Home

Chapter Five

Finally Home with Mom

This time when we arrived at the club, a beautiful brunette broke into tears as we handed her the cute little gift bag. She asked why we were giving her something because she was not used to kindness like this. I told her we gave her the bag because she was worth it. Her eyes welled and she said, "God sent you just for me. Right before you walked in, I called my mom to tell her I was ready to end it all. She told me to hold on because God has angels watching over me. I hung up the phone and…" the tears began to fall now, "…here you are." I hugged her, and began to tell her about the time God sent some angels for me. The day my father put me on a train and sent me off to what I thought would be a better life.

I arrived at the train station in Florida and dragged my garbage bags across the pavement to the little bench because the bags were too heavy to carry. I sat there for an hour, waiting for my mom to pick me up. I didn't have any money and I didn't know her phone number. I thought maybe my father gave her the wrong time, so I made a collect call to my dad's and he wouldn't

He wouldn't accept the collect call.

accept it. I was sixteen, alone, in a strange place, with my entire life in a bunch of garbage bags.

An older couple saw me crying and came over to me. It all poured out in a rambling, teary story. I didn't know my mom's address but I did know the name of her town, and I knew she had a bunch of Chow dogs and that there would be a swing set in the yard for my little sister.

With just that information, the couple grabbed my bags and put them in their car. I felt safe with them, with their kindness, their understanding. We drove for a bit, then they turned right and I saw a house with Chows in the yard and a swing set in the back, as if I'd created it out of my words.

I ran to the door and knocked, sure this was a dream, that it wouldn't be my mother on the other side. But it was, and she looked…stunned. She had no idea I was coming. My father lied. He never called her, just put me on the train and forgot about me.

Put me on the train and forgot about me.

I soon settled into a very different life at my mother's place. There was always food to eat, anytime I wanted. My mother gave me an allowance, so I could buy my own things. My mom had almost no rules, which was probably not a good thing. I went from living in an abusive, strict home to having free reign.

My stepfather was a truck driver and on the weekends when he was home we'd go to the local speedway where he was still racing cars. There, I met one of his friends, who was in his thirties. My stepdad and mother encouraged a relationship with him, even though I was only sixteen. I was allowed to stay over at his house, and even though I was underage, we'd have sex and he would proclaim his love for me, but in reality I was more like a showpiece. I didn't fit in with his friends or his world, but no one said anything. I have no idea how my mom was okay with this or why she didn't step in and stop it, especially when she saw me walking in with hickeys all over my neck.

When I was in 11th grade, I got a job at McDonald's. Gene would drive me to work, and even though he had a nice car, I was embarrassed to be seen with this older man.

I finally ended the relationship with him, and immersed myself in my friends and my new life. My new best friend, Tasha, and I partied with the seniors and spent a lot of time drunk. I still had feelings for Bill, and talked to him often. One weekend, he made the drive down from South Carolina and asked me to marry him. I didn't know how to handle this — how to accept that someone would love me that much. So I rejected him, and sent him back to South Carolina.

My mom gave me a beat-up old car which I called the Blue Hornet. One night, she and I had a fight. She threw a frozen steak at me that broke a mirror and in the midst of that fight, she fractured my ankle. Tasha and I loaded our clothes up in the Blue Hornet and ran away for a few days. Eventually, I came back home and my mom acted like nothing had happened.

In so many ways, I still didn't have a mom. She was more of a friend than any kind of parent. Then one day, she got a call from my father, saying his boyfriend had left him for another man (probably because he couldn't take any more abuse). My father was heartbroken and wanted to return to Florida. My life was about to change all over again.

I still didn't have a mom.

I was so far away from God and faith during that time. I was a wild child, who had given up on God, and whose life was spiraling out of control.

Chapter Six

Bouncing Between Homes

"Why are you doing this?" A skinny brunette girl stood before me in a dingy, dark, floral-scented dressing room that looked the same as all the others I had been in over the years. She was barely twenty, and already had the exhaustion in her eyes that said she'd been on that stage for far too long. She clutched the miniature purse I'd handed her, with tears welling in her eyes. "I don't understand."

I came closer to her. "Because I know where you are and where you can go from here."

She shook her head. "Where can I go? I'm going nowhere. I've got two kids, no education and no options. My life is a black hole."

I knew that feeling, knew the desperation in her voice. I heard myself in her story, as she talked about getting pregnant because she just wanted someone to love her, how the father of her children had disappeared, how she'd come from a home of addiction, where neither parent cared or wanted her. "I left that black hole," I said softly to her, "and you can too."

I left that black hole.

Those first few weeks at my mother's house were a bright light in a lot of long, dark years. Just as things seemed good, my father moved in. I felt like I'd just gotten away from him and wham, here he was again. My mother fell back into the old pattern of caving to whatever my father said and wanted. When he brought home a hitchhiker one night, he wanted me to share my bed with that stranger. I don't know if anything happened because almost all my memories around my father are blank spaces. Being near him always kicked my disassociation into full gear.

I had remained friends with Shelly, and as soon as I had enough money for a ticket, I hopped a train back to South Carolina and moved in with her. I got a job at a BBQ place called Rush's and we had our own apartment. At first, we lived in a two-story townhome where Shelly, her boyfriend and my ex all lived. We were all broke, and pretty much existed on ramen noodles and beer. Shelly was quite a pro at stealing and taught me to bring wire cutters into a store to steal clothes. We'd try them on and cut the security tag off, then stuff the clothes into a bag we had carried into the store. We stole everything — food, beer, cigarettes, and so on. Thank God we never got caught because my life would have been entirely different if I'd ended up in jail.

Life with Shelly was about partying. I tried mushrooms for the first time, and they gave me crazy hallucinations, which was the last thing I needed. I ran out of the house and sat on the grass alone, watching all the flowers dance and talk to me.

All the flowers dance and talk to me.

Sexually, I went down even darker roads. Shelly's boyfriend talked us into a threesome, and even though neither of us wanted it, we tried. Halfway through, Shelly got upset, so we stopped. But that didn't stop her boyfriend from coming on to me. He would line up sex toys on the bed whenever he and I were home alone, inviting me in to be with him. I threatened to tell Shelly, but he didn't care.

I remember having a panic attack when I thought I saw a black mass descend over me while I was home alone one day, one of those evil spirits my father had always claimed would punish me. I was so lost in those days, having sex with older men I barely knew, stealing from every store I went into, and partying almost every night.

Finally, I reached out to Bill. He came to see me, but he was very cautious about getting involved with me because of what had happened in Florida when I rejected him. For a while, he was there, rescuing me one night when I was so drunk, my friends had me on the kitchen floor and were trying to feed me bread in order to absorb the alcohol. Bill carried me to the shower, trying to sober me up. He tucked me safely in bed and I passed out. He was gone in the morning and unlike almost every man I had ever met, he didn't take advantage of me. He was such a good guy and I have always regretted what happened with him in Florida.

Things got so out of control that I eventually told Shelly I just couldn't afford to live there anymore and I bought a train ticket back to Florida.

My friend Tasha had gotten pregnant while I was gone and a few months later, she gave birth to a son. I stayed with my mom for a while (my father had moved into his own house by then) but eventually went to live with Tasha and her sister. But the pattern I started with Shelly happened here too — Tasha and I met some guys, moved in with them, and then started doing drugs. We dropped acid, which left me with crazy hallucinations. It's probably the worst drug I ever did.

My boyfriend got into trouble for robbing people's homes and went to jail. I moved back in with my mother, and went to stay with my dad off and on when things got bad at my mother's house. My dad was the same as always, taking me out drinking, letting me bring home older men, then sometimes trying to get those men to go to bed with him, too. My father was fascinated with my boyfriends, asking me intimate questions, wanting to see pictures of their naked bodies — I knew it was wrong, but it was my normal. I woke up one night on the couch to hear my father in his bedroom with my boyfriend at the time. I remember so little of those times because I disassociated as much as possible so I didn't have to face the darkness in my life.

When I was eighteen, my dad got me a job as a bartender. He took me clothes shopping before my first day and talked me into the skimpiest clothes we could find in the store. Before I left for work that night, he reached into my shirt and adjusted my cleavage, telling me that was how I was going to make good money.

I started going further off track, going home with one guy after another, agreeing to go in the back of the bar and perform sex acts on some of the male entertainers. Just writing this makes me break into tears. I know none of those men wanted me for who I am. To them, I was just an object to be violated time and time again. I had been used this way for as long as I could remember, and I don't think I even knew how to say no.

I don't think I even knew how to say no.

At every place I went, though, there was always at least one person who was a real friend. The cook's son was one of those people. He would stay after the club closed and make us cheese sticks and chicken fingers. We'd sit in the back and talk. It was nice to be with someone who wanted nothing more than friendship. This new friend ended up being much more in my life later.

The club owner started thinking of new ways to make money, setting up a hot dog stand in front of the club and having one of us girls man it while wearing a tiny bikini. Next, he hired female dancers to come in and strip. One girl called in sick one night and the owner asked me to fill in. I had to strip down to pasties and a thong, which honestly didn't seem that much worse than the tiny bikinis I'd been working in at the hotdog stand on the side of the road.

I remember feeling this strange mix of shame and empowerment. I hated that the men were grabbing me, rubbing up against me and shoving money at me, but I also liked making so much money. Like everything else, stripping would become my new normal and I just kept on moving forward, trying not to think about what I was doing or what it was doing to me.

Then I started noticing that my clothes weren't fitting right. Someone joked that maybe I was pregnant. I thought that was impossible, but three tests later, there was no denying it — I was going to have a baby.

My mom was shocked but somewhat supportive. She let me stay in her duplex in Bartow, but I had to keep working and pay my share of the bills. My father, on the other hand, wanted me to have an abortion. I never even considered that option.

Wanted me to have an abortion.

I finally had someone in my life who would love me, and whom I could love in return. I vowed to be a really good mom, and to make sure my child never wanted for anything and was never abused.

I lost my job, and I ended up losing all of my yearbooks and photos when we were evicted from the duplex in Bartow. My life was a mess, my self-esteem was zero, and I was about to bring a baby into this mess of a life. But I had hope for my child, and that was about to change everything.

Chapter Seven

Baby's First Home

A month later, my team and I enter another club. It's the middle of the day, the club is empty, and the girls are just sitting on the stage, talking. As we connect with them, I notice one girl sneak off to the dressing room, and as she passes, I notice her small baby bump. That breaks my heart because I know that was me years ago. When I talk to her, she tells me she's only eighteen, pregnant, and scared. She tells me she wants to get out of this life, she doesn't want to have to do degrading things in the private rooms just to make money. Her story could have been mine — a sexually abusive father, foster care, rape…

I hug her and begin to tell her how alike we are. I start talking about being pregnant with my first child, and how my life went from bad to worse during what should have been a time of great joy.

I lived with my mom, her girlfriend, my little brother and sister in a really nice apartment. I found out I was having a baby girl and because I was barely making any money, I applied for food assistance. That would take care of my salt and vinegar chip, pickled sausages and Twix® cravings.

> My entire life was in garbage bags.

It seemed appropriate that my entire life was in garbage bags because I felt like such garbage on the inside. As for God…I couldn't understand this loving being called "God" that people in church talked about because I was feeling the opposite of love from Him.

I started dating a really nice guy named Matt. We talked so much, and I started to fall in love with him. Too late, I found out he was fifteen, and I was just turning nineteen. But he was nice to me, and I was getting more scared the closer it got to my delivery date, so I kept on dating him. We talked about getting our own place after the baby was born. Matt's mom took me under her wing, teaching me to save and how layaway worked and how to plan for the future.

My mother and Matt's mother, along with my grandmother, held a baby shower for me. I was so caught in the fantasy and excitement of buying baby clothes and setting up a crib that I never took a second to think back and figure out who the father was. I narrowed it down to one boyfriend, but it didn't really matter — he wasn't there my entire pregnancy and didn't care.

I went into labor on February 22, 1993. It was a long, painful labor, twelve hours of serious pain. They finally gave me Demerol, which helped.

Then my father showed up and started yelling at the nurses, cursing them out for giving me anything for pain. My mother surprised me, though, jumping up and yelling at him to leave me and the nurses alone. You see, he didn't allow her any pain medicine with my two brothers and I. She understood.

When my daughter was finally born, my mom got to cut her umbilical cord. Then the nurse put my baby in my arms. Right away, I was so in love with her. She was perfect — dark-skinned with a beautiful full head of dark hair and blue eyes. In that hospital room, I had so many dreams that we would have a great life. I looked down at her tiny face, with her sweet fingers wrapped around mine, and I promised her I would make her life so much better than mine.

Make her life so much better than mine.

I had a lot of issues with breastfeeding and eventually had to switch to bottle feeding. When my father found out, he told me I shouldn't have any more children because I was clearly a bad mother if I couldn't do something as simple as breastfeeding. My mother and siblings helped sometimes with the baby, and adored her, so I tried to focus on them and not my father's judgmental words.

A few weeks later, my father was arrested for sexually abusing my little sister and one of my brothers. In that twisted, complicated relationship I had with him, he contacted me and told me that if I didn't get my siblings to recant, he would hang himself and his death would be all my fault.

His death would be all my fault.

Ordinary people might just say, let him do it. But my father had this weird control over me. I'm sure it was from the abuse, satanic control he had over me along with the hypnosis. I couldn't just walk away. He knew how to work that guilt factor, and before I knew it, I had talked my siblings into recanting.

The state, however, was still sure he did something. They made him register as a sex offender and complete years of probation and rehabilitation classes. I was humiliated and angry, all at the same time. Now my daughter had a grandfather who was a registered sex offender.

Meanwhile, my mother's apartment got so crowded, now that she had added my sister and brother to the mix. I knew I needed to find my own place, but I had no real skills, no real education. I went back to the one job I knew would give me a reliable income — stripping.

I'd been groomed for this path my whole life. I didn't see another route, any other options. To say I was broken would be an understatement. The only place I could gain acceptance was through my sexuality.

> Gain acceptance through my sexuality.

The degradation killed me inside a little every single day. I auditioned to *Purple Rain* and was hired. I hated myself and hated what I had to do, how I had to act and how I had to lower myself just to grab a pile of bills off the stage to feed my baby. I hated when friends would come in when it was my turn on stage.

Then I made a friend at the club who made it all easier. She gave me cocaine and told me that the coke would make me forget about what I had to do. She was right.

I remember sitting in the dressing room one night, snorting coke so I could go out there to strip and make enough money to provide for my daughter. I thought God didn't even know I was alive. How could He let me end up here, and drag my child into this horrible life?

Chapter Eight

Homes that Became Hells

I saw the blonde one more time that month. She was exiting the private dance room, clutching a thick stack of bills, and adjusting the tiny amount of clothes on her body as she moved across the room. She glanced up at me, and gave me a watery smile that said I'm sorry. All the times we talked, she promised to call because she desperately wanted out of this life. But she didn't call, and I knew why. The life had sucked her in, **with** its promises of easy money. But the degradation ate away at her soul, and told her she wasn't worth saving.

Watery smile that said I'm sorry.

Any other person might have given up on her but I couldn't. I stopped her in the hall and asked her how she was doing. Tears filled her eyes; she shook her head. I reached out and hugged her. I didn't say a word, I just hugged her, letting her know that I understood and I was there whenever she was ready.

I wish I had met someone like that earlier. I was this blonde years ago, when I started stripping and then moved into doing other things for money. In one night, I went from being a stripper to being, essentially, a hooker. It happened so fast I didn't have time to think or say no.

The girl at the club who gave me drugs then gave me $50 to drive her places. She said it wasn't bad at all, that she was never hurt by anyone and she just made a ton of money for very little work. I figured it would be okay, so I did my hair and makeup, and put on my best dancing outfit from the club. I was told she was doing private dances for bachelor parties.

Her boss told me it was time for me to see if I could make the cut with "the regular" guy they sent the girls to. I was determined to do that; to prove I was just as good as the other girls. I just had no idea what making the cut would mean.

When I get there, I realized "the regular" was a short pudgy bald-headed man who looked sleazy. I slipped into my Cayla persona, the one I adopted for dancing, and took the $250 he handed me.

I called the boss to tell her I was there, and she said I better be done in forty minutes and back in the car, and to make sure I gave them their half of the money. I glanced at the regular, and he was leering at me and rubbing himself. Things started to look much different than I'd thought. I should have listened to that still small voice that told me to say no to this. But now it was too late.

I started dancing, praying that was all he would want, but then he pulled me onto his lap and started running his hands all over me and under my outfit. I just wanted to cry.

I managed to convince him to not have sex with me, and instead to use my breasts. When he finished, he said, "Aww, baby, that was good. I'm going to have to see you more frequently."

I ran to the bathroom and scrubbed my face and chest so hard, I almost drew blood. Then I put on a smile, said goodbye to him and went down to the car. I met the boss down the street to give them their part of the money.

Before I could even get out of the parking lot, my pager went off and the boss sent me to another call. All totaled that night, they sent me on nine calls. One was at a well-known, fancy golf course. When I got there, I saw five men and realized I was going to have sex with all of them.

That night, they sent me on nine calls.

One after another, they came into the room, had sex with me, and then called out to the next one, "Buddy, you're up." I felt so degraded and broken. That was one of the lowest moments in my life, and I just wanted it to end.

I snorted some coke and that made it all easier to take. When I was done there, I went to another call. By the time I get there, I'm angry that I have to hand half of my money over to the boss. I'm the one being used, I'm the one being humiliated.

I'm the one being humiliated.

That night, I learned to hustle the customers. To take too much time talking to them so they would pay for another hour, or convince them that anything more than dancing cost extra money. When I was done, I would head to the bathroom and scrub myself raw. I would have a thousand dollars in my purse, but I couldn't look at myself in the mirror.

The next day, the boss told me she had more calls lined up for me. I tried to tell her no, that this wasn't what I wanted to do, but she just laughed. She told me I had no choice, and if I refused, she would get me blacklisted from all the other clubs and then tell my family what I had been doing. She told me I wasn't worthy enough for a regular job and would make sure everyone knew I was a hooker.

I didn't want my little girl — the baby I had done all of this for — to know what her mother had done to keep a roof over our heads. I couldn't live with myself, but I also couldn't live with the people I loved, knowing how low I had sunk.

My life became a hamster wheel of working at the strip club during the day, working for the boss at night, getting a few hours' sleep, then getting up and doing it all over again. The strip club was my drug money and I used the other money for bills and fancy things for my daughter.

It became harder and harder to hide the truth from Matt. I would stop at a gas station on the way home every night and get all cleaned up and pray he wouldn't figure it out. To deal with all of it, I started doing more drugs.

I tried to satisfy the customers without intercourse, but they would demand it or hit me if I didn't comply. I ran into angry girlfriends and once an angry mother who came running out of her room with a rolling pin. I can't tell you how many times I had to grab my stuff and run out of the house half-naked.

One night, I went to the house of a guy who seemed "off". He kept pressuring me to say I was there for sex but I knew something wasn't right. I just kept telling him that was illegal and that I was there to do lingerie modeling. Next thing I knew, there were cop cars pulling into the yard. The guy took off, but the cops kept me there for questioning. I stuck to my story that I was there to be a lingerie model and they finally let me go. As unhappy as the boss was that I got caught, they praised me for not making a mistake.

I was under their control for three years until I became pregnant again with my son. They let me go then, thank God. I was still dating Matt, who was the father of my son, but after the baby was born, waitressing wasn't paying the bills and my roommate's boyfriend was constantly trying to put his hands on me.

I wanted my daughter to be safe for me to be safe. The only way I knew to afford that and to survive was to go back into the life I had left. My little sister lived with me and she would watch the kids while I was being sent out. I had pretty much stopped working at the strip clubs and was now solely being prostituted. I went from boss to boss, some of them better than others. One had me smuggle crack in my bra into the Bahamas, then used me as his personal toy while we were there.

Solely being prostituted.

I became highly addicted to pain pills and tried coming off them. I was put on Methadone, which was just trading one drug for another. I'd nod off between jobs, losing myself a little more each day. I would then begin smoking crack to keep me awake while on the medication.

Losing myself a little more each day.

I was so broken and became very promiscuous, even when I wasn't working. I desperately wanted someone to love me. I ended up getting pregnant by a guy who was on a football scholarship and didn't want a child. I was in no position to have another one. I felt like I had no other choice but to have an abortion. I wanted to die when I laid on that table, listening to those horrible sounds, knowing what I was doing. I justified it in my head, like I justified everything else, telling myself this would allow me to take care of the two kids I had. I got pregnant again later, after a spring break trip filled with drugs. I had no idea who the father was, and once again, chose an abortion.

A year later, I started having extreme pain in my abdomen. I was rushed to the hospital to have my appendix removed. When I woke up from surgery, the doctor told me he almost had to give me an emergency hysterectomy because of the infection. He asked me if I had ever terminated a birth. I told him I had a year earlier, and he said that the clinic that did the abortion had left me with an infection that was brewing for a year.

Here I was, in my twenties, having a partial hysterectomy. I thought this was God's way of punishing me for all my terrible choices.

God's way of punishing me.

I finally found my daughter's father. He wanted nothing to do with her but I begged him to be a part of her life. The agreement was that I would let her go there for a summer to get to know him. Her father found out about my lifestyle and tried to do everything in his power to keep her from me. We argued after every visitation and I finally told him I was filing for custody (we had worked out an arrangement between ourselves, so there was no formal custody arrangement in place). That same night, the police showed up at my door with a restraining order for me, from my daughter's father.

The police took my daughter away from me. I can still hear her screaming, begging me to not let them do that. My heart broke because I couldn't do a thing about it. We went to court and I was slapped with an indefinite injunction, which meant I could only have supervised visitation. I had lost and failed my sweet girl, my baby, and my first child.

I was so lost and hated myself so much during that time. I ended up getting involved with a man who dealt drugs and gave me an endless supply of cocaine. It was a toxic relationship — he would cheat, we would fight, then we'd snort coke together. I just did more and more cocaine because every time I came down, I'd have to face the mess of my life.

I started mixing in other drugs to take the pain away: pain pills, Xanax, ecstasy. I overdosed one night and felt like I was going to die. I asked my boyfriend to please let my kids know I loved them and laid there helpless as I felt myself drifting further away. In my head, I prayed, begging God to let me live while promising to never again do drugs.

I did live, but I didn't stop doing drugs. Cocaine had lost its appeal for me, though, and I never enjoyed it like I had before. I broke up with my boyfriend and went to work in a lingerie shop where my older sister was working. It turned out it was just a fancy name for a brothel. The customers would come in, pick a girl, then go in the back and do whatever they wanted. The owners found out we were sisters and capitalized on that, often sending us to bed with the same customer. It was too much! We were sent to a strip club together to be featured entertainers. Our father was there to support us. I drank so much that night; it was all so incredibly overwhelming.

I was pulled over that night and charged with DUI. The state took my kids. My daughter went with her father (he had allowed me to see her from time to time) and my son went with a family member. I was charged with child endangerment and I remember begging them, sobbing, telling them that my life was nothing without my kids. I was labeled suicidal and put in a cell with nothing in it except toilet paper and a metal bed with no covers. That was one of the most miserable nights of my life and all I could think about was the mess my life was and my children.

When I was released, I vowed to live differently, but I was too broken and filled with so much self-hate, that I went right back to the old habits of drugs, partying, and running to calls. I kept telling myself the court wouldn't sentence me and I could go back to my life. I could fix it all.

I was wrong. At my hearing, I was sentenced to 60 days in jail. I broke down in court. My life was a crazy, unfixable mess. It felt like I was falling down a rabbit hole and there was no way out. I was sure that God was angry with me, and doing everything He could to punish me.

60 days in jail.

Chapter Nine

Jail Becomes Home

So many of the girls I talk to have been to jail, or live in fear of going. It's one of the things that bond us when we talk because I know how bad it can be. I remember talking to one girl who had just gotten out of jail and went back to stripping the same day. She knew nothing else, and couldn't see a world where she lived a normal life. We talked for hours, sitting in a diner drinking crappy coffee. When we finally said goodbye, I could see hope in her eyes. I talk to dozens of precious girls a week, and as much as I wish they all saw themselves as being able to get out, the reality is that only a handful can break free from that life and that pain. Don't get me wrong; these are strong women, I was a strong woman, but that life takes ahold of you.

Life takes ahold of you.

I get that. When I went to jail, I thought my world had ended. I faked a pregnancy by getting urine from a pregnant friend just before I went to jail, so I could keep getting methadone. The doctor saw me every week, and started to get suspicious when my stomach didn't get any bigger. I contracted MSRA because the jail was so filthy. A week before my release, the doctor wanted to do an internal exam because he couldn't detect a heartbeat. I knew if they did that, they would discover that I had no uterus or cervix and that I had been lying. I managed to talk the doctor into letting me go to my own doctor when I was released the next week.

Jail was so depressing. I was there over Thanksgiving and became so depressed that I wasn't with my kids. A group of ladies from a church told me I could have a better life, but I couldn't hear them. They left me with a King James Bible and I would read it all the time, even though I really didn't understand the words on the page. There were seeds being sown in my heart by God, even though I couldn't see them.

After I was released, all I wanted was my children back, but the state refused. I had Section Eight benefits and was in jail when the state came to do my home inspection. I lost my place and had to move in with my brother. I began to spiral again. I went back to drugs and when I got tested at my probation meeting, I failed. I had screwed up again and I knew my son wasn't coming home anytime soon. My heart broke and I held him so so tight when I dropped him off that night.

I tried, I really did. I got off the methadone and went into serious withdrawal. I ended up being sent back to jail for violating my probation. I lied to the guards and the doctor again, saying I had miscarried. My life was nothing but a big lie and vicious circle of one bad thing after another. By the time I was released a few weeks later, I had no home to return to and no place to go.

I begged my mother to let me stay with her. I had to have an address to report to probation or I'd be sent back to jail. My mom agreed but told me I would have to follow her rules, starting with finding a real job. I caught the bus and started looking for waitressing jobs. While at the bus stop, I ended up getting picked up by a trick. I was desperate for money. I never told anyone how I ended up with money.

I found an ad for phone work that was close enough to the house for me to ride my bike there. I had no idea what I was getting into until I listened in on a call and realized it was a sex hotline. I told myself it was better than stripping and prostituting.

I told my mom about the job, but instead of nurturing me or telling me not to do it, she laughed it off. I came up with four different characters that I would play on the phone. One of them was a dominatrix. The enemy would whisper in my ear and tell me it was my turn to hurt the men who had hurt me, to belittle them. Those whispers fueled something in me. I had a true hatred for men and I was now walking into dangerous territory where I would feed the beast.

To hurt the men who had hurt me.

I made enough money to move into a crappy duplex. I prayed every night for my son to come home, for my daughter's father to give me visitation. I became desperate for money to pay the bills, get food, pay off my DUI fines, buy a car, and then get custody of my son again. I ended up working for an escort service that sent men to my house. I had nothing but an air bed where I would have to see sleazy, stinky men in my own home. I met a girl at the phone sex call center, and she convinced me to do this from home, using a webcam. We set ourselves up on an adult site and I began to do live camera sessions as a dominatrix. Then I began to meet my subs for live sessions. I made an incredible amount of money, got my life in order (or so I thought), jumped through all the hoops for the court and finally brought my son home.

I thought I could handle it. I told myself that I would work at night when he was asleep and we'd be a happy family the rest of the time. It didn't quite work out that way. He had major behavioral issues from all he had been through and I didn't know how to handle it. I'd become very easily frustrated. One night, I couldn't keep him inside and went so far as to grab him and bite his lip in my frustration. This mistake still sits very well in his memory and writing this breaks my heart. I went back to my old friends — alcohol and drugs. I was determined to make things right, but instead I kept making bad decisions.

Kept making bad decisions.

I managed to pay off my fines, get my license back and buy a car. I needed my daughter in my life again, so I worked hard to make enough money to move us to Brandon, where she was. I was still a mess, but telling myself every day that I was doing okay. I still had that Bible, and even though I felt tremendous shame and guilt, I was beginning to think maybe there was a God and maybe I could find Him, and in the process, find myself.

Part Three: Building Home

Chapter Ten

Finding a Home in Church

Like so many of the women I see and counsel, change doesn't happen overnight. There's so much more involved in finding the strength to leave, to move on to a new and different life. For me, like the women I sat and cried with and hugged, change took time to settle into my heart and my life.

My daughter was living with her father, and even though I lived close enough to see her often, her father and I had a rocky relationship. I kept up the webcam business, and doing real-time sessions. I went back to popping pain pills to manage the guilt that was killing me.

Popping pain pills to manage the guilt.

The injunction was lifted and my daughter was allowed to decide where she wanted to live. She had a big fight with her father over that, and chose to live with me, even though her father and stepmom had told her about all the horrible things I was doing.

I tried to slip into a normal life. It was her homecoming weekend and we went shopping for the pretty dress and sparkly shoes, like a regular mom and daughter. I even took her to see her dad. She was so beautiful and wanted him to see her, to accept her. Instead, he told her not to come back. He rejected and abandoned her for coming home to live with me. As you can imagine, my daughter had many behavioral problems. I had no idea how to be a good mother because I had no role model for that.

One day, I got a call from the high school to come and get my daughter, who was wasted on Xanax. I felt like a failure but kept telling myself I was fine. I even made her get up and go with her friends and family to a theme park in that drugged-out state because I was too ashamed for them to see what a failure I was. I was always trying to prove myself.

We moved to a big house — I kept thinking another home would somehow fix things —and I thought we were fine. My son was in middle school and my daughter in high school. I was making a lot of money. My kids had the best of everything, I was getting my hair done in an upscale salon, tanning daily, driving a new car a customer bought for me, and thinking I had arrived.

But to make that money, I was still doing the calls. I'd do it while the kids were at school and thus unaware of what I was doing, or so I thought. Without my knowledge, my daughter would skip school, sneak into the house and sleep in her closet. She overheard so many of those calls I made or heard me bringing a customer into the house for a session. Even today, it kills me to think about what I put her through.

My son was in baseball so we were at the baseball field on a regular basis. I really didn't have any girlfriends because I was so consumed by work, my pills and my kids. But I made friends with one of the moms at the baseball field. She was so different, leading a normal life, and I looked up to her. One day, she invited me to church. I had only been to church once in my adult life for a funeral, and I was so sure that Jesus wanted nothing to do with someone like me and that the church would burn down if I walked into the building. But I was good at playing the part and said yes for all the wrong reasons. I wanted to look like the good baseball mom, and went.

From the second I got out of the car, I was sure everyone could see what I was covering up, and that they would judge me and kick me out. I sat with my friend and her family, nervous, scared, and ready to bolt.

Nervous, scared, and ready to bolt.

Then the service started. The stage is lit up, people are singing and it's more of a show than a preachy hymn. As the music continued, I felt something come over me. I began to weep.

I listened so intently to the pastor and his message. When he finished, he asked if anyone there wanted to accept Jesus into their heart. I raised my hand and walked to the front of the church. He handed me a paperback bible and praised me for making Jesus my savior.

I began digging into that paper bible and going to church every weekend and every first Wednesday. I bought a life journal and was inside that church almost every time the doors opened. I began volunteering wherever I could. My son joined the youth program, but my daughter wanted nothing to do with the church and that was probably because she knew what a hypocrite her mother was.

I would pray and go to church, and in between, I still worked the webcam and took customers. I couldn't tell anyone that I was still working in the sex industry. I was sure they would kick me out if I told the truth.

Inside, I was beginning to change gradually. I upgraded to a study bible. I stopped cursing. I sought

God's word more but my life was still out of control. I felt like I was wearing three masks — sex worker, mother and Jesus believer — and I was exhausted.

> I was wearing three masks.

My father was diagnosed with tongue cancer and I was the only one in the family that would have anything to do with him. I went to church to have him prayed for on the morning of his surgery. One of the pastors was walking by and stopped. He said to me, "Someone has cursed you and placed many things on you." I now know that it was my father the pastor was referring to.

After my father's surgery, he stayed with us for a little while. He was still the same mean man even as he said he was a very spiritual man who knew everything about the bible. Remember, he was the leader of a satanic group. This explains why he hid behind God and knew scripture better than anyone. It was his cover up for his flaws and an excuse for his behavior.

Meanwhile, my daughter fell in with the wrong crowd. She'd sneak people into her room at night, get alcohol and party with them. My room was on the other side of the house and I would either be working or too zoned out on pills to even notice what was happening.

I met with my son's youth pastor's wife, and she helped me, even though I barely opened up. I had cut back on working, and couldn't afford the house anymore. We moved into a crappy trailer for a while. My son began getting into trouble and I had no control over my daughter. I'd never been the disciplinarian I should've been. I never wanted to abuse them like my father had done to me. Add in the drugs and my own guilt, and it was a recipe for disaster.

Still, I kept trying. I would get so frustrated; all I knew to do was call the police to help me control them.

Many times, they would be taken to DJJ, also known as the kids' jail/detention center. Many times, I would be visiting my children in jail because I didn't know how to handle them and they were broken along with me.

They were broken along with me.

We moved into a better home and neighborhood, because I thought that would change everything. But it didn't. My daughter's father called Child Protective Services and they took her to foster care. The shame about my life began to hit me hard. I wasn't a good mother; I was still working in the sex industry and abusing prescription drugs.

The more I dug into the Word, the more I realized how messed up my childhood and life had been. Even as I battled shame and regret, God started planting a dream inside of me. If I ever got out of the industry, I wanted to help other women who were caught in this awful cycle.

Then one night, I got too drunk when I was out on a call with a customer that I couldn't pick my son up. I asked his friend's mom from church to let him stay overnight. I was so ashamed of what I had done and how far my life had gotten out of control that when I got home, I took a handful of pills.

I called my kids, begged them to forgive me, and then laid down to die. I passed out on the front doorstep. My son's friend's mom showed up to bring my son home and when she found me and woke me up, I broke down and told her I needed help.

Passed out on the front doorstep.

She called an ambulance, and I opted to voluntarily check myself into a mental hospital for a few days. I ended up leaving as quickly as I got there. Anxiety was in full effect and I wanted to go home. Guilt was eating me alive. I would think of times I asked my daughter to take pictures of me in lingerie so I could place them on my site. I thought of how many times I had let my kids down or had done horrible things just to survive.

I prayed and prayed for a way out of my life. I kept thinking about a sermon I had heard where the pastor said we needed to bring things to light in order to heal. I had no idea how to do that. I tried reaching out to the church but was always shut down and told I couldn't speak to the pastor I wanted to see. I would close back up, but I yearned for freedom.

So, I prayed and God listened. I sat down at my computer one night and thought maybe someone else had figured a way out. I did a Google search, typing in "women who love Jesus but are in the sex industry support group". I almost fell out of my chair when an organization in California called Treasures popped up on my screen. I put in all of my information and was instantly set up with a mentor. They sent me a care package full of books, including Harmony Dust's book *Scars and Stilettos*, and Joyce Meyers' *Beauty for Ashes*.

Those books changed my life. I finally saw that there was a way out, a way to forgiveness. Hope was beginning to rise in me. I opened up to my mentor and told her the truth. She encouraged me and never judged me. "Christa, your story is like the story of Joseph," she said one time. "You have been imprisoned your whole life but God's about to give you the land like He gave to Joseph." I held onto that and read Joseph's story in the Bible over and over. She shared with me how big churches worked and with her encouragement, I reached out to the church and asked to speak to one of the pastors on the pastoral care team. It didn't matter anymore who it was, I trusted her. I was stepping out of my life and into the light for the first time ever. I was desperate for help and wanted freedom so bad. I couldn't chance attempting suicide anymore.

I couldn't chance attempting suicide anymore.

Chapter Eleven

An Almost Unbearable Month at Home

When I sit down with these women in the clubs, I see it like giving a testimony in church. I'm unbundling my past to them, allowing them to see that I have gone through the same fire as they have, and I have found a way to emerge victorious. My road was rocky — just as the road has been for so many of these girls — but the common bond we create in these conversations in back rooms and dim hallways create a framework for when the girls decide they want out of the life. I feel like I'm putting a ladder before them, and each conversation puts in one more rung. After that, it's up to them if they want to climb up or not.

I'm putting a ladder before them.

The first time I gave a testimony was in a letter. I had read Joyce Meyers' book and was so astounded at what she had survived, that I sat down and wrote my own story out. I mailed it to her, and although I have no idea if she received it or read it, simply telling my story opened that locked door in my mind. It was enough to allow me to let people around peek inside at all the things I had kept secret for so long.

When I met with the pastor at the church, I took that testimony with me. I was terrified of what he might think of me and I figured it would just be easier to read than to have a face-to-face confession. I sat in his office and started reading. Tears streamed down my face. When I finished, I sat in the soft, cushioned chair and waited for his response. I expected judgment. I expected him to throw me out.

He took a breath. "We love you," he said. "Jesus loves you and we're going to walk with you through this season of your life."

Walk with you through this season of your life.

I cried. All of my life, I had felt like I was unacceptable, not good enough, not lovable, and here was this pastor, who hardly knew me, giving me acceptance and grace for all the horrible things I had done and had done to me. He didn't tell me to leave the industry but instead gave me all kinds of tools and groups to join, like Celebrate Recovery and Job Finders. He sent me home with encouraging videos and would send me other encouraging ones by email.

After that day, he began to counsel my daughter and I and even wrote a letter to the courts on my behalf so I could bring her home. With God's help, I argued successfully in court and brought my daughter home. After that, the church set us up with a professional counselor, and continued our meetings with the pastor.

The church helped us a lot. They gave us gift cards for gas and food and they helped pay the bills I couldn't cover. Job Finders helped me with a resume, which was fabulous because I had a pretty lean job history. If I added up all the real jobs I worked over the past twenty years, I had maybe a year of total employment time, so we had to get creative. To explain the time gap, we said I owned a business. I did, and we said I worked in sales. I had; it was just a different kind of sales.

I became a co-leader at Celebrate Recovery after knowing I would have my own ministry for women in my situation. Prior to speaking to my Pastor, I had reached out to Treasures that summer and finally found some kindred souls who understood what I had gone through. That gave me the courage I needed to reach out.

That fall, Joyce Meyers came to town. I was broke, and really couldn't afford to take the time off, but I just knew I couldn't miss the conference. I'm glad I didn't because this was the game changer for me.

Joyce started sharing the story of the prodigal son. It's the story in the Bible about two sons. One runs off and squanders away everything his father gave him, while the other son stays with the father and is considered the good son, the righteous one.

When the prodigal son returns home, his father welcomes him with open arms and throws a party for him with the best of everything. Just as this father welcomed his son who had sinned and disappointed his father, so does God welcome us when we return to Him too.

As Joyce was sharing this story, I could hear God whispering in my head and I saw a vision of Him on that stage, holding His arms out to me saying, "Come on, Christa, you can do this. I love you and I am your provider, not that industry."

I am your provider, not that industry.

In that moment, I had a revelation of His deep love for me and that was all it took to change the course of my life. My mom was there with me and I told her that I was going to write up my story of why I was leaving the industry and post it on the adult site where I worked. She reminded me that I had $70 dollars to my name. But, I didn't care — I knew that God would provide. On November 21st, 2010, I shared my story, with my real name and my real age of thirty-seven. I wrote a long letter about why I was leaving, telling everyone that it was Jesus who freed me and that I was doing what God had told me to do.

Almost instantly, other women posted on the site, thanking me for inspiring them and encouraging them to leave. Men who were once customers began to email me and share how badly they struggled with their faith while participating in calling girls and doing phone and camera sessions.

I began to minister to those men, and I realized how many of them had come from abusive households themselves or had religion forced down their throat so much that they rebelled as much as they could against it. They gave me money — not for the sex acts I had done before, but to support me and to thank me for helping them.

But there was more I needed to change. December 6, 2010, I heard God tell me that it was time to put all my prescription pills down at the foot of the cross. I wasn't abusing them anymore but my body still needed them first thing in the morning. I took my last dose of pain medication that day and also my last dose of Xanax. Two days later, my body was withdrawing so violently my son called the ambulance and they rushed me to the hospital. The doctor in the emergency room told me it was dangerous to come off that amount of medication cold turkey and that I could die. He wanted to wean me off the meds with smaller doses, but I refused and told him that God had me. I didn't want or need any substance to do this.

God had me. I didn't want or need any substance.

The doctor told me there was nothing else he could do and released me. I lay in my bed for well over a month, severely ill. I slept in little catnaps of ten minutes at a time. I couldn't eat and was vomiting constantly. I laid there and prayed over and over again, reminding myself that, "I can do all things through Christ who strengthens me."

I can do all things through Christ who strengthens me.

The detox was horrific. I began to hallucinate, and forget how to do basic things like wash my hair. I went to the doctor again, but by then I was so far into my own detox that there wasn't anything he could do. He suggested I call a detox center. I returned home and did. They told me the same thing: I was too far through my withdrawals and it would be dangerous for them to touch me. After that call, feeling hopeless, a friend from church called me and said she just wanted to tell me that God had told her to remind me He was my physician and I was coming out of the wilderness soon, and going into the promised land. I wasn't instantly better but that was the hope I needed.

I don't recommend anyone coming off the amount of medication I did without help unless you are clearly hearing from God. This was not an easy time; in fact, it was one of the hardest moments of my life. However, God knew me better than I knew myself. He knew I wouldn't be able to do it by weaning myself down a little bit at a time. I was the kind of addict who had to be all in or nothing.

A couple of months after I gave up all the drugs, I went to a friend's house for dinner. It was so weird being out in society without being fogged up with Xanax and every other drug I had been on for over ten years. Everything was different — driving my car was like learning to do so all over again. Church was overwhelming with all the people so I'd get social anxiety sometimes.

Our Christmas that year was lean because I was still pretty broke and hadn't found a job. However, it seemed like God sent some money just when I needed it most. We weren't living large, but we were making it, day by day. I knew God had us in His hand. Those months were probably the sweetest time I have ever experienced with Jesus and the first time I didn't stress out over a bill. I would get up and have my coffee on the back porch with Him and just walk around in awe of Him, talking to Him. I also did a lot of listening to Him.

The miracle of God was incredible. I hadn't paid rent since October, but my landlord never said a word. Our electricity never got cut off and although we lost our cell phones, all of our other needs were met, right down to toilet paper. He handled it all for almost four months. I knew I had to do something and God led me to my closet. Last year's income tax return fell out of nowhere, this was it, this was my answer. I was so sick I had forgotten all about filing. I filed and right when my return was accepted, the landlord's patience ended! I got a three-day notice to vacate and my money arrived! We were able to move.

I told a friend at church about some duplexes I had seen. She happened to work with the lady who owned them. That lady ended up taking a chance on me even though I had no income, a criminal record and multiple evictions.

I worked part-time painting houses, moving furniture, anything to pay the bills. Then I took a job selling continuing education to CPAs. That money was a blessing. I moved on later to work in sales at an air conditioning company. I had to learn everything from scratch — how to work the printer and all the software. I faked it until I knew what I was doing because I was determined to make this work.

I was determined to make this work!

My journey wasn't easy and not without mistakes. Those mistakes, however, ended up shaping me in new **ways** and taking me to a whole new level in my faith.

Chapter Twelve

Building a Forever Home

The first time I went into a strip club after leaving the industry was probably the hardest. I was there with Strip Church and Treasures, handing out little bags with lip gloss in them, along with some hope. I went in with such optimism but as I stood there in this crowded club, I lost sight of the woman who was in charge of our group.

I faltered. *Look at you, you can't even follow the leader*, my mind whispered. *You mess everything up; there is no way you will be able to do this.*

At that moment, one of the other women in our group came up to me and we asked one of the girls if there were more women in the dressing rooms. There we found our leader, because the girls had pulled her into the room to talk to her. My friend was just as nervous as me and together we went to the back. I handed a bag with the lip gloss in it to one of the girls and she asked me what she owed me. I said she owed me nothing — that we did this to let them know they are important and loved.

They are important and loved.

As we walked out of the club, the DJ gave us a shout-out and several of the girls thanked us. The door shut behind me, and I realized in that moment even more why I was called to reach these precious women. The next day, we continued training and in that training, I realized that I was a victim. I had gotten caught up in sex trafficking, too. Up to that point, I don't think I'd fully accepted that truth.

I came back home, pumped and ready to start Loving You Where You Are At, the name God gave me for the ministry He was trusting me with. I thought of all kinds of girly, catchy names but the Lord gave me that one. I started a Facebook page and started meeting with a few people but as much as I tried, I couldn't seem to get traction. I talked to the pastor and he encouraged me to keep going but to beware of the spiritual warfare the enemy would wage against my work, and how he would tempt me to fall into old ways.

Around this time my father's cancer got worse. The surgery they did failed, and he suffered through major doses of radiation and chemotherapy, but it wasn't enough. He had contracted HIV, and his cancer had moved to his lungs; he was dying.

For years, I had worked on forgiving him because I knew the importance of forgiving. I finally did, shortly before the end of his life. I moved him into my dining room and had hospice come in and my kids and I sat by him and kept him company in those long, dark days.

Then one night, when the three of us were there, he said to me, "I was just remembering one of our sexual escapades." For a second, I thought he was delusional, and reminded him that I was his daughter. But then a wave of shame come over me and I knew that he was talking about things he had done to me, things I had forgotten and buried deep inside me.

I ran out of the room, curled into a ball on my bed, sobbing as memories flashed through my mind. I begged God to please stop them, telling Him not now, I couldn't handle it. The memories stopped, but I knew I had to make a change when I got up in the morning.

I wanted to put my father into a hospice center. He was triggering memories in me, and they would have the ability to give him round-the-clock care. I cried myself quietly to sleep. It was beginning to be too much taking care of him, working and trying to get the ministry going. On top of that, he also still wasn't a very nice man to my kids.

Wasn't a very nice man to my kids.

In the end, my father got sick, ended up in the hospital, and the doctor sent him to a hospice home. My brothers came to see him, and I assume made their peace with him. My sisters came and so did my mom, each taking time to see him.

We wheeled him around in his wheelchair and took him out to the garden so he could have a smoke and look at the flowers, something he loved to do. He once told me that you could see God everywhere, even in the flowers. He also loved to listen to spiritual music with his headphones, and that day, I could tell the end was close. He sat in that wheelchair and started to stare at the flowers like he was taking everything in, memorizing it. Then he pulled out his phone and put his headphones in as if it was one last time. He played *I've Got You, Babe,* from Sonny and Cher, and he and my mom sang together to the song they had played at their wedding. My dad moved his wheelchair around with his feet like he was dancing. It was a nice, sweet moment.

When we got back to his room, he pulled me aside and told me not to give up my ministry. It was such a mixed message from the man whose abuse had been a major factor in me ending up where I was. I now know that was another part of his manipulation. You see God called me but He wanted me to have a few years to learn who Christa was, what Christa liked, to have a few years of a normal life, and to do more healing. My father only pushed that because he knew the hold he had on me. He knew I would jump right into ministry when God wanted to give me some time.

He died the next morning, alone, at 6 A.M. When the nurse called, I rushed up there and found his cold body tucked nicely in his bed. He looked so at peace. Maybe for the first time in his life.

During all of this, my daughter got pregnant. I think getting pregnant was her saving grace. She was working at a job that involved traveling door to door, selling cleaning supplies. In my opinion, it was labor trafficking. My daughter fell into drugs; I even did drugs with her at one point in her life and there were times we would have full-on fist fights. I am still working through the shame and guilt of this. I always think if only those things hadn't happened, would she have been at that job? Thankfully when she found out she was pregnant, she didn't touch drugs again.

My sweet granddaughter was born premature and spent two weeks in the NICU. With a fuller house, we moved into a bigger place. I was still working and trying to get my ministry off the ground. I asked God if maybe I had it all wrong because nothing seemed to be moving forward.

Shortly after that, I received a phone call from a lady who ran a homeless shelter. Many of the women who came to her were involved in prostitution and she wanted to be better equipped to help them. We met several times and she decided to join me in outreach. I was nervous because I knew consistency was important and once we started doing this, it would be something we had to do every month. We prayed about where God would have us go and He led us to Pasco County and Tampa. I had no clue why He was sending me an hour away to Pasco County, but later, I realized He had a reason.

Our first venture into the clubs was in December of 2013. I was so nervous but didn't want to show it. I needed to be bold like I had been trained to be. We met so many amazing women, and so many who were highly addicted to drugs. Nevertheless, we had many God moments that night and saw many tears.

After I shared some of the pictures on my Facebook page, things began to expand. Women from local churches called and asked if they could donate, including two from a church in Dunedin, which was where I was born. Then others asked to join our ministry. Within a couple months, we were up to eight people on our team, which meant we could add more clubs and reach more women.

We would take the women gifts, along with our card that let them know they were "Loved, Valued, and Purposed," and support was only a phone call away. We would take baked goods to the male staff.

Loved, Valued, and Purposed.

Before I knew it, there were so many people who wanted to get involved. I had to host another training at the Church in Dunedin. Isn't it funny how God picked that church to be so supportive, considering Dunedin is the city I was born in? Only God could do that! He was giving me back the land just as my mentor had said He would. I have also gone into both detention centers where my children were previously housed to speak to female youths who have been identified as being trafficked or at high risk. It was so different going into the very places I used to visit my kids, but for very different reasons. God was redeeming everything.

God was redeeming everything.

We split our outreach up into two nights; Wednesday night would be Tampa while Thursday night would be Pasco County where we divided into two teams to cover all the clubs in a timely manner. Up until then, I was funding the ministry entirely from my own money. I was working full-time, trying to run the ministry and feeling overwhelmed.

I dropped down to part-time work, to have a couple of days a week for outreach, but I soon realized I wasn't making enough money to support my family and my ministry. "I don't know what to do," I told God. "I can't do both but how will I survive? The numbers just don't make sense." He gave me a clear vision of a girl sitting on a dock just dipping her toes in the water. When I looked out across the lake, He was holding His arms out, telling me to just jump in the water and trust Him, so I did.

From that day on, I found a way to raise enough money for the ministry and still pay my bills. When I shared this story on Facebook, one of my friends who was also a part of a ministry in the area told a woman she knew (who was still working in a club) what I did. That woman told my friend to tell me to go buy five loaves of bread and two fishes and watch what God would do. I did and they sit in my freezer to this day. When I bought them, I had no idea how powerful God was going to turn out to be.

Go buy five loaves of bread and two fishes and watch what God would do.

Chapter Thirteen

A Home for All

I went back to the blonde one last time, and this time, with an offer. "I'm in the process of opening a home where women can stay, while they get on their feet and get out of the life." She stared at me, as if I was speaking another language. Then she said softly, "A home?"

I nodded, hugged her, and gave her my personal number. When I left, I wasn't sure if I'd see her again. She was sporadic about being there when I came in, and I was worried that she was going to end up leaving before I could help her.

One day, she showed up at the drop-in-center, her belongings in a small bag by her side. She looked scared and unsure, but I invited her in to take the first step into a new, better life. Our home has not opened yet, but I placed her in another safe place until we can open "The Butterfly House".

My road to getting here wasn't easy. I started panicking every time I had to speak and experiencing serious anxiety all the time. God spoke to me in a dream. He showed me there was an obstacle keeping me from moving forward. I knew what that was. I broke down and reached out to my friends, who pointed me in the direction of a psychiatrist who would help me pro bono. The doctor was stunned at all I had been through. She diagnosed me with complex PTSD, something women in the commercial sex industry experience at rates equivalent to combat war veterans.

She diagnosed me with complex PTSD.

She prescribed medication for me and recommended that I start seeing an EMDR therapist to deal with the trauma. I felt so broken and defeated when I went to the pharmacy to pick up my medication. I had vowed long ago that I wouldn't take another pill. I was afraid that maybe God didn't think my faith was strong enough or big enough but then I realized that it was okay to use medication to get through this. I had been through a life of hell that caused severe trauma and there was a reason God made doctors. If you are reading this and struggling like I was, *please know it is okay to get help.*

Please know it is okay to get help.

Am I completely healed? No, it will probably take a lifetime to work through those thirty-seven years of hell. But my panic attacks are pretty much gone and my anxiety is under control.

Our team started praying for a drop-in-center, a place where the women we were reaching could come for survivor-led support groups, one on-one mentoring, resources, and much more.

God came through. The church in Dunedin that had been so instrumental in the beginning was asked to take over a dying church in Pasco County that was within walking distance to one of our clubs. God knew all along why He sent me an hour away to start my ministry.

We later started another one at a safe house that the Salvation Army in Tampa had set up. I found I loved working with the girls. We had so many tears and laughs in those groups, along with a lot of healing. Girls were praying, accepting Jesus and getting baptized.

The key is that we treat these precious women like any other women. We have normal conversations and Jesus conversations. We go in loving them with no strings attached and they know it. We love them even if they don't believe in Jesus. Our job is to love, and let the Holy Spirit do the rest. We never tell them to leave the club or criticize their choices. They will make those decisions when and if they are ready.

Through my speaking engagements, we were becoming known for our work. We even received a proclamation from the Pinellas County Board of County Commissioners for our work with Human Trafficking. Talk about a redemptive moment! In my previous life, I ran from police and now I was standing next to them, being applauded for my hard work.

Being applauded for my hard work.

Still, I felt like God wanted me to build a safe home for women like me. I'd gone almost all my life without a real home of my own; a place where I belonged. I didn't know of any place I could go when I was in the life and I knew there were very few for other women. Even though it is the number-two crime in the world, there are less than 300 beds for sex trafficking victims and less than 200 are for women over eighteen.

We found our house in 2017 and named it The Butterfly House because we believe the women who come here for our year-long program will leave as a new person, ready to spread their wings and fly.

We are raising money to run it; no small task, because it will cost us about $200,000 to run it annually. We know God will provide and while we wait for Him, we continue our monthly outreach.

As I've watched these women's lives be transformed, so too has my own. My mom was inspired by how I accepted Jesus and began to search the Word for herself. My siblings and I still talk, but maintain healthy boundaries. My brothers and I remain close even though they live out of state. I am so proud of where they are, considering all we went through.

God has really moved in restoring the relationship with my children. Things aren't perfect, but we have rebuilt our relationship and are mending the damage done by those years when I was an addict and working in the industry. My daughter even became part of my ministry's team. She did end up stepping away at a certain point because it's hard for her. I also realize there is still so much healing to happen for my children. That has to happen in their time and I know God will redeem all things by helping them heal in His perfect timing.

My precious granddaughter is now four and brings me great joy. I love that little princess in ways I can't even explain. It's almost like a do-over. I get to make the right choices with her and nurture her in ways I wasn't able to nurture my kids because I wasn't in a healthy place for so long.

My kids were what kept me going through those hard years. I wanted so badly to become a mother they were proud of and worked so hard to get to this place. I am far from perfect and I know there is still so much more healing to be done. All I can do is pray God continues to work in me and through me and show me how to be the best person I can be.

Loving You Where You Are At, the foundation, is my biggest achievement and one that I hope will change many more lives. We are more of a love-based organization than faith-based, because in the end, it all comes down to love. To me, Jesus is the love that resides in all of us, making our hearts His home.

I found my home in Him. I found myself in Him. And I have found my purpose in this life in Him.

I found my home in Him.

To anyone reading this, I want you to know there is hope for any situation. There is a great plan for your life and you will make it through. You are loved by such a deep love right where you are, as you are.

Where is God? He is right there, with you, waiting for you to take His hand and walk the journey He has prepared for you. I promise, you will find love, hope, and home at the end of that path.

Chapter Fourteen

Where God Was

As I've written this book, I have tried to look back and see where God was, how he was nudging me or looking out for me during these difficult times of my life. I may have thought He didn't care about me but He did. He was there — He was always there — and when I look back, I see the ways that God tried to reach me and comfort me.

Early in my life, I can see how He protected my mother from being killed by my father. He also gave me the strength to get through those awful childhood years. And He gave me some good and precious memories to hold onto when things got dark and bleak.

Jeremiah 29:11 says, "For I know the plans I have for you" declares the Lord, "plans to prosper you and not to harm you, plans to give you hope and a future." I held on to that verse a lot over the course of my life.

God was with me in that scary house where I lived in with my father, protecting me from the evil that was happening. Yes, I had to see and endure terrible traumas, but looking back, it could've been so much worse. He also sent along another worker who interrupted that molestation at the elementary school. And He gave me that brief time with my mother. My father hid his satanic involvement by using God and religion, but God protected me from a lot of the satanic stuff.

Later, He tried to protect my siblings and I by sending DCF to our house. Our fear drove all of us to lie, which almost cost us that help we so desperately needed. Regardless of the outcome, He made sure my siblings and I weren't separated and maybe that was because we would desperately need each other in the years to come.

As I got older, my anger at God grew because I felt like He had abandoned my siblings and I many times. But He was there all along, protecting us from a life that could have been so much worse. All that time, He was fighting against the darkness that surrounded us. God was at war for us but I was too angry to see it.

Then when I was at that train station, God was the one who sent angels to rescue me; angels who knew where my mom lived and who helped me out when I needed it most. Only God could do that. He had His hand on me that entire journey.

God always made sure I had a roof over my head. I could have ended up homeless and living on the streets but I didn't. He also gave me just enough strength to endure that horrific introduction to stripping. And He blessed me with a reason to see my future in a new way — my child.

He gave my siblings the courage to speak up and rescued them from more abuses coming from our father. He saved their lives. He placed a great Christian woman in my life, my boyfriend's mom, and because of her, seeds of faith were being planted. Seeds that would soon bloom and change my life.

The night I almost died, God saved me, but I thought it was because I bargained with Him; I didn't realize He did it out of love. He protected me from getting seriously hurt at many calls with customers. He protected me from getting that prostitution charge and protected my kids and I from dying the night I received my DUI. He was there, even though I wasn't seeking Him and struggling to have any faith at all.

He protected me in that jail and showed me grace, even when I didn't deserve it. He helped me learn about Him with that Bible and He brought my son back to me. It was then that I began to become receptive to God's messages. He began to make his presence known and helped me start to believe that maybe, just maybe, He loved me.

He brought a believer friend into my life and sneaky Jesus got me. I went everywhere for all the wrong reasons but God knew just what I needed and where I needed to go. He was breathing life over me and placing a deep calling in my heart. When I wasn't even aware of it, He was giving birth to something in me that would redeem so much the enemy had taken. It's taken a long time, but it is now very clear to me where God was. I knew Him and I had a relationship with Him. My father hid behind God. While I was growing in my relationship with Jesus, my father was trying to manipulate me and twist my relationship with my Heavenly Father. He did crazy things like holding an actual blood sacrifice of a goat, held right above my body. He and the other people in his satanic group threw curses at me, saying I would be a bride of Satan and a server of man. God protected our sacred relationship and allowed me to hear Him louder than my father. Even as I was serving men and living that life, God protected me, saved me and made me a bride to Jesus.

Now He has brought my calling full circle, giving me the tools and people to save so many women from the life I lived. Every single day, He reminds me of His promises and has me step out in faith a little more, always showing me that He was and is my provider. He has called me to this ministry and He will provide.

God has always been there in my life, even when I couldn't see Him or hear Him or even believed He existed. If you are struggling with your faith, with knowing that God loves you just as you are, try getting quiet and simply talking to God. He is there and He is listening and just waiting for you to come to Him.

Where to Go from Here

If you are caught in this industry and are looking for help and resources, please contact Christa at:

LOVING YOU
WHERE YOU ARE AT

www.lovingyouwhereyouareat.com

f www.facebook.com/lywyaa

t twitter.com/lywyaaChrista

You will also find assistance at:
www.iamatreasure.com

About the Author

Christa Hernandez is the founder and executive director of Loving You Where You Are At. Her organization was founded in October, 2012 after attending training with Strip Church and years of envisioning a survivor-led outreach to women in the commercial sex industry. She is a survivor of almost twenty years of childhood  sexual abuse, sex trafficking and work in the commercial sex industry. Loving You Where You Are At currently visits 12 strip clubs across the Tampa Bay area every month, bringing them the reminding message that they are Loved, Valued, and Purposed. She is passionate about making known the issues surrounding sex trafficking, sexual exploitation and sexual abuse as well as sharing the hope she found in Jesus to overcome.

In 2016, she received a Human Trafficking proclamation from the Pinellas County Board of Commissioners for the work she does. She is also a public speaker, sharing her story and awareness on sex trafficking.